Freedom Press

9mm M 9 Semiautomatic Pistol Owner's Manual

The Following is a U.S. Army Manual without Copyright released to the General Public.

They are provided for informational purposes only.

ISBN-13: 978-1508978961

ISBN-10: 1508978964

FAIR USE ASSERTION

Any materials used in this book to illustrate and assist in comprehension, have been used under the Fair Use Copyright assertion of Section 107

Section 107 contains a list of the various purposes for which the reproduction of a particular work may be considered fair, such as criticism, comment, news reporting, teaching, scholarship, and research. Section 107 also sets out four factors to be considered in determining whether or not a particular use is fair:

- The purpose and character of the use, including whether such use is of commercial nature or is for nonprofit educational purposes
- The nature of the copyrighted work
- The amount and substantiality of the portion used in relation to the copyrighted work as a whole
- The effect of the use upon the potential market for, or value of, the copyrighted work

The distinction between fair use and infringement may be unclear and not easily defined. There is no specific number of words, lines, or notes that may safely be taken without permission. Acknowledging the source of the copyrighted material does not substitute for obtaining permission.

The 1961 Report of the Register of Copyrights on the General Revision of the U.S. Copyright Law cites examples of activities that courts have regarded as fair use: "quotation of excerpts in a review or criticism for purposes of illustration or comment; quotation of short passages in a scholarly or technical work, for illustration or clarification of the author's observations; use in a parody of some of the content of the work parodied; summary of an address or article, with brief quotations, in a news report; reproduction by a library of a portion of a work to replace part of a damaged copy; reproduction by a teacher or student of a small part of a work to illustrate a lesson; reproduction of a work in legislative or judicial proceedings or reports; incidental and fortuitous reproduction, in a newsreel or broadcast, of a work located in the scene of an event being reported." Copyright protects the particular way authors have expressed themselves. It does not extend to any ideas, systems, or factual information conveyed in a work.

ARMY TM 9-1005-317-10
NAVY SW 370-AA-OPI-010/9mm
AIR FORCE TO 11W3-3-5-1
MARINE CORPS TM 1005A-10/1
COAST GUARD COMDTINST M8370.6

OPERATOR'S MANUAL

PISTOL, SEMIAUTOMATIC, 9mm, M 9
(1005-01-118-2640)

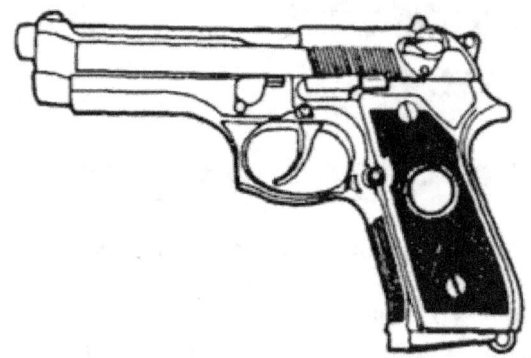

DEPARTMENTS OF THE ARMY, NAVY AND AIR FORCE.
COMMANDANTS, MARINE CORPS AND COAST GUARD

JULY 1985

CHANGE

DEPARTMENTS OF THE ARMY, NAVY, AIR FORCE HEADQUARTERS, MARINE CORPS AND COMMANDANT, COAST GUARD

No. 3

Washington, DC   14 December 1990

Operator's manual

PISTOL SEMIAUTOMATIC, 9mm, M9
(1005-01-118-2640)

ARMY TM 9-1005-317-10, NAVY SW 370-AA-OPI-010/9mm, AIR FORCE TO 11W3-35-1, MARINE CORPS TM 1005A-10/1 and COAST GUARD COMDTINST M8370.6, 31 July 1985, is changed as follows:

1. Remove old pages and insert new pages as indicated on the next page.

2. New or changed material is indicated by a vertical bar in the margin of the page.

3. Added or revised illustrations are indicated by a pointing hand indicating area of change,

Remove Pages	Insert Pages
1-7/(1-8 blank)	1-7 thru 1-9/(1-10 blank)
2-25 thru 2-28	2-25 thru 2-28
3-19 and 3-20	3-19 and 3-20
None	3-22.1/(3-22.2 blank)
3-23 thru 3-26	3-23 thru 3-26
4-1 and 4-2	4-1 and 4-2
D-3 and D-4	D-3 thru D-5/(D-6 blank)
Index-1 and Index-2	Index-1 and Index-2

4. File this change sheet in back of this publication for reference purposes.

TM 9-1005-317-10, C3

By Order of the Marine Corps:

H.E. REESE
Deputy for Support
Marine Corps Research, Development and
Acquisition Command

W.T. LELAND
Rear Admiral, USCG

DISTRIBUTION:

To be distributed in accordance with DA Form 12-40E,
(Block 610), Operator's Maintenance requirements for
TM 9-1005-317-10.

TM 9-1005-317-10, C3

By Order of the Secretary of the Army:

CARL E. VUONO
General, United States Army
Chief of Staff

Official:
JOHN A. FULMER
Colonel, United States Army
Acting The Adjutant General

By Order of the Secretary of the Air Force:

MERRILL A. McPEAK
General, United States Air Force
Chief of Staff

Official:
CHARLES C. McDONALD
General, United States Air Force
Commander, Air Force Logistics Command

CHANGE

DEPARTMENTS OF THE ARMY, NAVY, AIR FORCE
HEADQUARTERS, MARINE CORPS AND COMMANDANT,
COAST GUARD

No. 2

Washington, D.C,   28 March 1989

Operator's Manual

PISTOL, SEMIAUTOMATIC, 9mm, M9
(1005-01-118-2640)

ARMY TM 9-1005-317-10, NAVY SW 370-AA-OPI-010/9mm, AIR FORCE TO
11W3-3-5-1, MARINE CORPS TM 1005A-10/1 and COAST GUARD COMDTINST
M8370.6, 31 July 1985 is changed as follows:

1. Remove old pages and insert new pages as indicated on the
next page.

2. New or changed material is indicated by a vertical bar in
the margin of the page.

3. Added or revised illustrations are indicated by a pointing
hand indicating area of change.

1

Remove Pages	Insert Pages
3-11/(3-12 blank)	3-11/(3-12 blank)
3-17 thru 3-20	3-17 thru 3-20
3-27 thru 3-30	3-27 thru 3-30

File this change sheet in back of this publication for reference
purposes.

CHANGE

DEPARTMENTS OF THE ARMY, NAVY, AIR FORCE
HEADQUARTERS, MARINE CORPS AND COMMANDANT,
COAST GUARD

No. 1

Washington, D.C, 10 July 1987

Operator's Manual

PISTOL, SEMIAUTOMATIC, 9mm, M9
(1005-01-118-2640)

ARMY TM 9-1005-317-10, NAVY SW 370-AA-OPI-010/9mm, AIR FORCE TO
11W3-3-5-1, MARINE CORPS TM 1005A-10/1 and COAST GUARD COMDTINST
M8370.6, 31 July 1985 is changed as follows:

1.   Remove old pages and insert new pages as indicated on the
next page.

2.   New or changed material is indicated by a vertical bar in
the margin of the page.

3.   Added or revised illustrations are indicated by a pointing
hand indicating area of change.

1

Remove Pages	Insert Pages
a and b	a and b
1-1 through 1-7/(1-8 blank)	1-1 through 1-7/(1-8 blank)
2-1 through 2-4	2-1 through 2-4
2-7 through 2-12	2-7 through 2-12
2-15 through 2-28	2-15 through 2-28
3-5 through 3-22	3-5 through 3-22
3-25 through 3-33/(3-34 blank)	3-25 through 3-33/(3-34 blank)
A-1 and A-2	A-1 and A-2
C-1 and C-2	C-1 and C-2
D-3 and D-4	D-3 and D-4
Index-1 through Index-4	Index-1 through Index-4

File this change sheet in back of this publication for reference
purposes.

By order of the Secretaries of the Army, Navy and Air Force; Headquarters, Marine Corps end Commandant, Coast Guard:

CARL E. VUONO
General, United States Army
Chief of Staff

Official:

R. L. DILWORTH
Brigadier General, United States Army
The Adjutant General

R. E. BROWN
Small Arms Program Manager
Naval Sea Systems Command

LARRY D. WELCH
General, USAF
Chief of staff

EARL T. O'LOUGHLIN
General, USAF
Commander, Air Force Logistics Command

J. J. WENT
Lieutenant General, USMC
Deputy Chief of Staff for
Installation and Logistics

C. E. ROBBINS
Rear Admiral, USCG
Chief, Office of Operations

Distribution:
  Active Army:
    To be distributed in accordance with DA Form 12-40-R, Operator's Maintenance requirements for Pistol, Semiautomatic, 9mm, M9
  Marine Corps:
    MARCORPS CODE BN
  Navy:
    Speci a l
  Air Force:
    Speci a l
  Coast Guard:
    IAW COMDT NOTE 8000

WARNING

Read this manual carefully before handling, loading, or operating the pistol.

Do not point pistol at personnel when loading, clearing, or firing as this could result in injury to, or death of, personnel.

For safety considerations, the hammer should always be lowered to the fully down position by depressing the decocking/safety lever.

The M9 pistol incorporates single and double action modes of fire. Anytime the trigger is pulled with the decocking/safety lever in the firs (up) position and a round in the chamber, the pistol will firs from the hammer down, half cock or full cock positions.

The decocking/safety lever can be moved to the fire (up) position with a minimum amount of force. This could happen during removal of the pistol from the M12 holster if carried in the safe (down) position and/or during careless handling.

WARNING (cont)

Make sure your pistol is clean. Before loading, inspect the barrel to ensure it is clean and free of foreign objects. Shooting with an obstruction in the barrel such as dirt, mud, grease, or lodged bullet could cause injury to the operator, or damage to the pistol.

Use only ammunition authorized in chapter 4.

Hearing damage may occur unless proper hearing protection is worn when firing the pistol.

For further information on safety, care, and handling of ammunition, refer to TM 9-1300-206.

For further information on first aid, refer to FM 21-11.

TECHNICAL MANUAL
NO. 9-1005-317-10
AVY SW 370-AA-0PI-0101/9mm
TECHNICAL ORDER
NO. 11W3-3-5-1
TECHNICAL MANUAL
NO. 1005A-10'1
COAST GUARD COMDTINST M8370.6

ARMY TM 9-1005-317-10
NAVY SW 370-AA-OPI-010/9mm
AIR FORCE TO 11W3-3-5-I
MARINE CORPS TM 1005A-10/1
COAST GUARD COMDTINST M8370.6

DEPARTMENTS OF THE ARMY, NAVY, AIR FORCE,
COMMANDANTS, MARINE CORPS AND COAST GUARD

WASHINGTON, DC, *31 JULY 1985*

OPERATOR'S MANUAL

PISTOL, SEMIAUTOMATIC, 9mm, M9
(1005-01-118-2640)

i

REPORTING ERRORS AND RECOMMENDING IMPROVEMENTS

You can help improve this manual. If you find any mistakes, or if you know of a way to improve the procedures, please let us know. Mail your letter or DA Form 2028 (Recommended Changes to Equipment Publications and Blank Forms) direct to: Commander, US Army Armament, Munitions and Chemical Command, ATTN: AMSMC-MAS, Rock island, IL 61299-6000. A reply will be furnished to you.

Navy users submit Recommended Changes to Publications to: Commanding Officer, Naval Weapons Support Center, Code 20, Crane, IN 47522-5020.

Air Force users submit AFTO Form 22, Technical Order System Publications Improvement Report and Reply to: WR-ALC/MMEDT, Robins AFB, GA 31098-5000.

Marine Corps users submit Form 10772 to: CG, Marine Corps Logistics Base, Code 850, Albany, GA 31704-5000.

Coast Guard users submit Publications Correction/Change Report form to: Commandant, U. S. Coast Guard, (G-ODO), Washington, DC 20593.

TABLE OF CONTENTS

TABLE OF CONTENTS (cont)

TABLE OF CONTENTS (cont)

CHAPTER 1
INTRODUCTION

1. FIRING PIN BLOCK
2. EXTRACTOR/LOADED CHAMBER INDICATOR
3. TRIGGER
4. FRONT SIGHT
5. SLIDE ASSEMBLY
6. DISASSEMBLY LEVER
7. SLIDE STOP
8. REAR SIGHT
9. DECOCKING/SAFETY LEVER
10. HAMMER
11. RECEIVER
12. GRIP
13. LANYARD LOOP
14. MAGAZINE (SEATED)
15. MAGAZINE CATCH ASSEMBLY
16. DISASSEMBLY BUTTON

Section I. GENERAL INFORMATION
9mm PISTOL

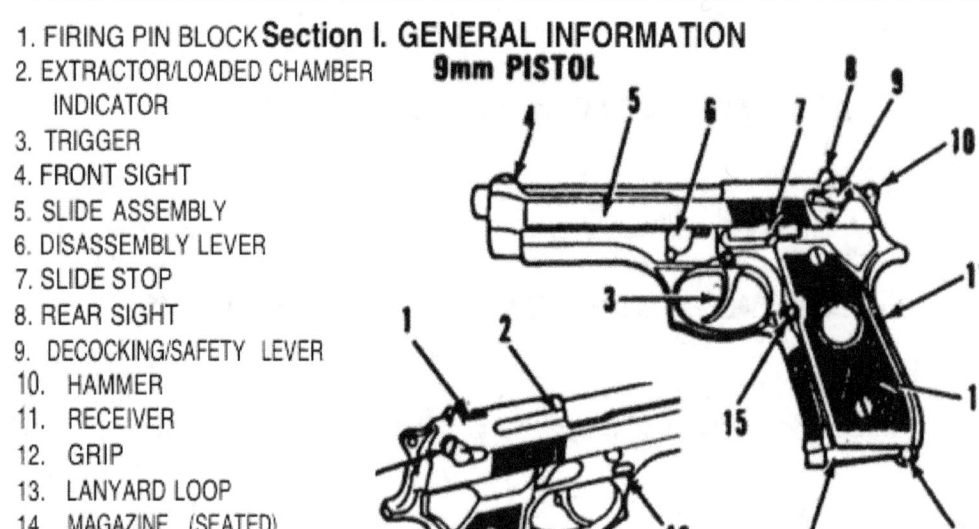

TM 9-1005-317-10

1-1. SCOPE.

a. Type of Manual. Operator's Manual.

b. Model Number and Equipment Name. M9 9mm Semiautomatic pistol.

c. Purpose of Equipment. Provides personal defense protection.

1-2. MAINTENANCE FORMS AND RECORDS.

Department of the Army forms and procedures used for equipment maintenance will be those prescribed by DA PAM 738-750, The Army Maintenance Management System (TAMMS).

USMC users refer to TM 4700-15/1 for applicable forms and records.

1-3. REPORTING EQUIPMENT IMPROVEMENT RECOMMENDATIONS (EIRs).

If your 9mm pistol needs improvement, let us know. Send us an EIR. You, the user, are the only one who can tell us what you don't like about your equipment. Let us know why you don't tike the design or performance. Put it on an SF 368 (Quality Deficiency Report). Mail it to us at Commander, US Army Armament, Munitions and Chemical Command, ATTN: AMSMC:(QAD, Rock Island, IL 61299-6000. We'll send you a reply.

Navy users submit Quality Deficiency Report to Commanding Officer, Naval Weapons Support Center, Code 20, Crane, IN 47522-5020.

Air Force users submit Material Deficiency Report (MDR) to: DIR MAT MGT ROBINS AFB GA//MMIRFT// and Quality Deficiency Report to: DIR MAT MGT ROBINS AFB GA//QAY//.

USMC users should submit SF 368 to CG, Marine Corps logistics Base, ATTN: Code 856, Albany, GA 31704-5000.

1-4. NOMENCLATURE CROSS REFERENCE LIST.

Common	Official
Magazine	Magazine, Cartridge
Extractor/Loaded Chamber Indicator	Extractor
Slide...	Slide Assembly
Magazine Release Button	Magazine Catch Assembly
Round	Cartridge
Decocking/Safety Lever	Safety w/Lever

1-5. DESTRUCTION OF MATERIAL TO PREVENT ENEMY USE.

Only your commanding officer can give the order to destroy material to prevent enemy use. Refer to TM 750-244-7.

1-6. NUCLEAR, BIOLOGICAL AND CHEMICAL (NBC).

Genaral procedures can be found in FM 3-4, FM 3-5 and FM 3-87.

Section II. EQUIPMENT DESCRIPTION

1-7. PRINCIPLES OF OPERATION

a. The M9 Pistol has a short recoil system utilizing a falling locking block.

b. Upon firing, the pressure developed by the combustion gases recoils the slide-barrel assembly. After a short run, the locking block will stop the rearward movement of the barrel and release the slidewhich will continue its rearward movement. The slide will then extract and eject the fired cartridge case, cock the hammer and compress the recoil spring. The slide moves forward feeding the next cartridge from the magazine into the chamber.

c. The slide and barrel assembly remains open after the last cartridge has been fired and ejected.

1-8. MAJOR COMPONENTS.

a. SLIDE AND BARREL ASSEMBLY (1). Houses the firing pin, striker, end extractor, and cocks hammer during recoil cycle.

b. RECOIL SPRING AND RECOIL SPRING GUIDE (2). Absorbs recoil and returns the slide assembly to its forward position.

c. BARREL AND LOCKING BLOCK ASSEMBLY (3). Houses cartridge for firing, directs projectile, and locks barrel in position during firing.

d. RECEIVER (4). Serves as a support for all major components. Houses action of pistol through four major components. Controls functioning of pistol.

e. MAGAZINE (5). Holds 15 cartridges in place for stripping and chambering.

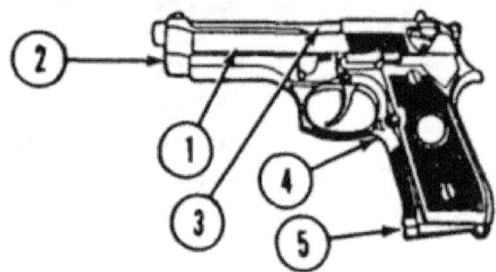

1-9. EQUIPMENT DATA.

Caliber	9x19mm(9mm NATO)
System of Operation	short recoil, semiautomatic
Locking system	oscillating block
Length	217 mm (8.54in.)
Width	38mm(1.50in.)
Height	140 mm (5.51in)
Weight (w/empty magazine)	960 gr(33.86 oz)
Weight(w/15 round magazine)	1145 gr(40.89 oz)
Barrel Length	125mm(4.92 in)
Rifling	R.H, 6 groove [pitch 250mm (about 10in.)]
Muzzle velocity	375 meters/sec (1230.3 ft/sec)
Muzzle energy	569.5 newton meters (420 ft.lbs)
Maximum effective range	50 meters (54.7 yards)
Maximum range	1800 meters (1969.2 yards)
Front sight	blade. integral with slide
Rear sight	notched bar, dovetailed to slide
Sighting line	158mm (6.22in.)

Safeties. . . . .– Manual decocking/safety lever, located on the slide, which separates the firing pin from the hammer, lowers the hammer when cocked, and interrupts the connection between trigger and sear.

– Firing pin block, prevents any motion of the firing pin and is overcome only by pulling on the trigger.

Hammer (half cock) . . . . .helps prevent accidental discharge

Magazine . . . . .staggered, 15 round capacity

Slide . . . . held open upon firing of last cartridge

Grips . . . . .plastic, checkered

1-10. CORROSION PREVENTION AND CONTROL (CPC).

Corrosion Prevention and Control (CPC) of materiel is a continuing concern. It is important that any corrosion problems with this item be reported so that the problem can be corrected and improvements can be made to prevent the problem in the future items

While corrosion typically associated with rusting of metals, it can also include deterioration of other materials such as rubber and plastic. Unusual cracking, softening swelling, or breaking, of these materials may be a corrosion problem.

Change 3   1-7

If a corrosion problem is identified, it can be reported using Standard Form 368, Product Quality Deficiency Report Use of key words such as 'corrosion", "rust", "deterioration" or "cracking" will assure that the information is identified as a CPC problem.

Army users submit Product Quality Deficiency Report (SF 368) to:

Commander
U.S. Army Armament, Munitions and Chemical Command
ATTN. AM SMC-QAD/Customer Feedback Center
Rock Island, Illinois 61299-6000

Air Force Users submit Materiel Deficiency Report (MDR) to:

DIR MAT MGT
ATTN; MMIBTC
Robins AFB, GA

and Product Quality Deficiency Report to:

DIR MAT MGT
ATTN. MMOA
Robins AFB, GA

Marine Corps Users submit Materiel Deficiency Report (MDR) to:

    Commanding General
    Code 808-1
    Marine Corps Logistics Base
    Albany, GA 31704-5000

Navy users submit either Product Quality Deficiency Report or Materiel Deficiency
Report (MDR) to:

    Commanding Officer
    Naval Weapons Support Center
    Code 20
    Crane, IN 47522-5020

Coast Guard users submit RAPIDRAFT letter (CG Form 3883) to:

    Commandant, U.S. Coast Guard (G-ODO)
    2100 - 2nd Street S.W.
    Washington, DC 205930001

CHAPTER 2
OPERATING INSTRUCTIONS

Section I. DESCRIPTION AND CHARACTERISTICS OF OPERATOR'S CONTROLS AND INDICATORS

2-1. DESCRIPTION.

The M9 pistol is a semiautomatic, magazine fed, recoil operated, double action pistol, chambered for the 9mm cartridge.

WARNING

The M9 pistol incorporates single and double action modes of fire. Anytime that trigger is pulled with the decocking/safety lever in the fire (up) position and a round in the chamber, the pistol will firs from the hammer down, half cock or full cock positions.

2-2. OPERATIONS AND CHARACTERISTICS.

a. DOUBLE/SINGLE ACTION. For double action, pulling the trigger will cock the hammer and immediately release it, discharging the first chambered round. To fire the first chambered round in single action, the hammer must be manually locked to the rear before pulling the trigger.All shots after the first one will be fired single action because the slide automatically recocks the hammer after each shot.

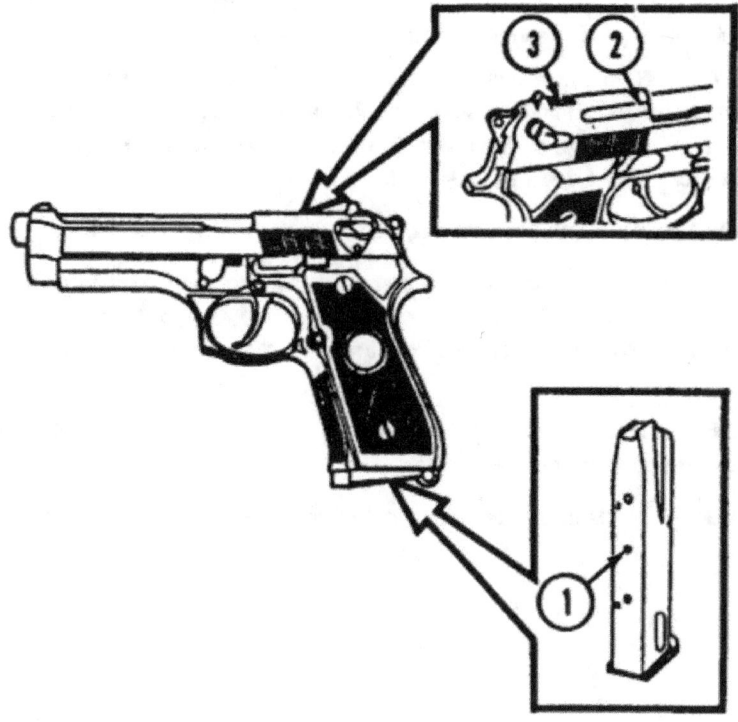

2-2

b. MAGAZINE (1). Has a 15 cartridge capacity.

NOTE

In non-tactical situation, visual inspection of the chamber is recommended.

c. EXTRACTOR/LOADED CHAMBER INDICATOR (2). When there is a cartridge in the chamber, the upper surface of the extractor protrudes from the right side of the slide. In the dark, the protrusion can be felt by touch. The loaded chamber indicator should be used in tactical situations when visibility is limited or where visual inspection of the chamber is desirable.

WARNING

A potential safety hazard exists if the firing pin block is missing or does not return flush with the slide surface after firing.

d. FIRING PIN BLOCK (3). When the trigger is not pulled, the firing pin block secures the firing pin and prevents it from moving forward, even if the pistol is dropped.

WARNING

The decocking/safety lever can be moved to the fire (up) position with a minimum amount of force. This could happen during removal of the pistol from the M12 holster if carried in the safe (down) position and/or during careless handling.

e. DECOCKING/SAFETY LEVER (4). Allows safe operation of the pistol by both right and left handed users, and lowers the hammer without causing an accidental discharge. Pistol is shown with decocking/safety lever in the fire (up) position. When hammer is cocked, it may be safely lowered by moving the decocking/safety lever to the safe (down) position.

f. LANYARD LOOP (5). Compatible with standard lanyards.

g. RECEIVER (6). The front and back straps of the grip are vertically grooved to ensure a firm grip even with wet hands, or under conditions of rapid combat fire. The trigger guard (7) is extended, and the concave forward portion is grooved for a firm grip when using two hands or gloves.

h. DISASSEMBLY LEVER (8) AND DISASSEMBLY BUTTON (9). Allows for quick field stripping, and at the same time prevents accidental disassembly.

i. SLIDE STOP (10). Holds the slide to the rear after the last cartridge is fired. It can also be manually operated.

2-4   Change 1

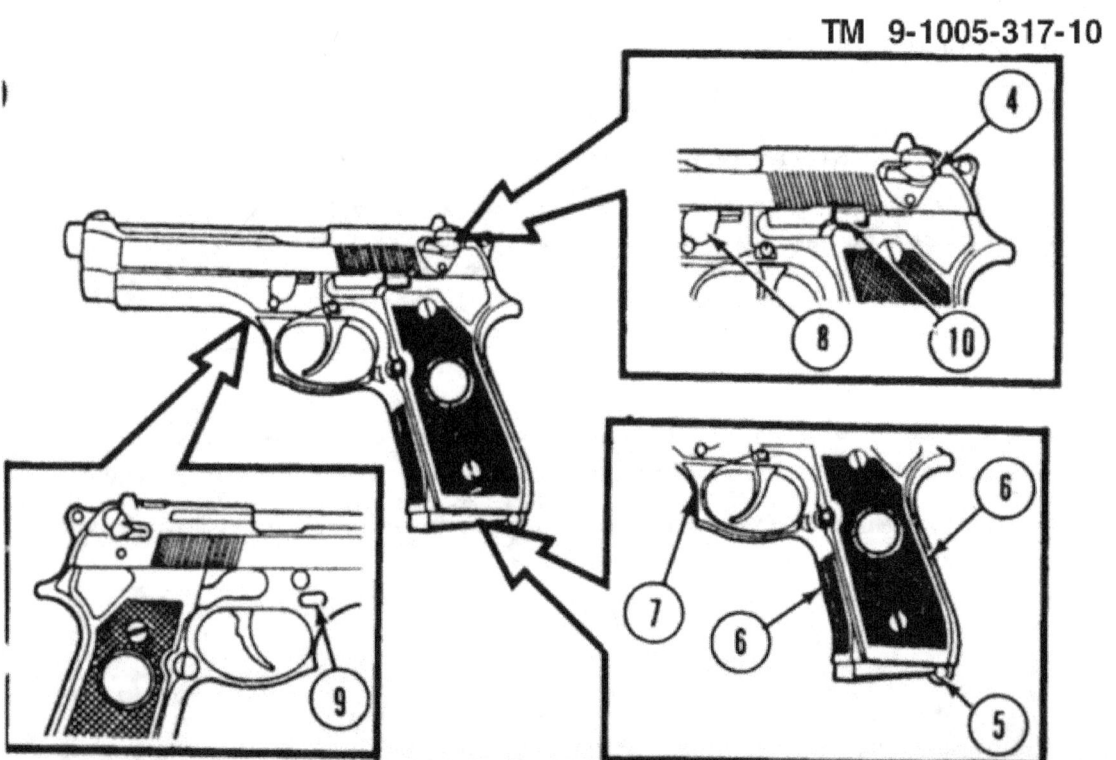

Section II. PREVENTIVE MAINTENANCE CHECKS AND SERVICES (PMCS)

2-3. GENERAL

NOTE

Always keep in mind the WARNINGS and CAUTIONS.

a. Before You Operate. Perform your before (B) PMCS.

b. During Operation. Perform your during (D) PMCS.

c. After Operation. Perform your after (A) PMCS.

d. If Your Equipment Fails to Operate. Refer to troubleshooting table in chapter 3. Report any deficiencies using the proper forms. See DA PAM 738-750.

2-4. PMCS PROCEDURES.

The PMCS table (p 2-9) lists those required checks and services to be performed by personnel who operate the M9 pistol. The table is divided as follows:

2-6

(1) Item No. Column. The numbers in the item no. column of the PMCS will be used as the item numbers for the TM number column on DA Form 2404, Equipment Inspection and Maintenance Worksheet. if anything looks wrong and you cannot correct it yourself, write it on your DA Form 2404 and notify your organizational maintenance RIGHT AWAY.

(2) Before Operation Service. This is a brief service to ensure the M9 pistol is ready for operation.

(3) During Operation Service. Periodically check to ensure the M9 pistol is functioning properly.

(4) After Operation Service. This service should correct, where possible, all operational so the M9 pistol will be ready to operate when needed.

5) Not Ready/Available If Column. The PMCS table also lists those deficiencies which make the M9 pistol not ready/available. They are listed in the right-hand column.

PREVENTIVE MAINTENANCE CHECKS AND SERVICES (PMCS)

WARNING

Before starting an inspection procedure clear the pistol. Inspect the chamber to ensure that it is empty. Do not keep live ammunition near work/maintenance area.

NOTE

See page 2-21 for unloading the pistol and magazine.

If equipment is NOT READY/AVAILABLE, evacuate the pistol to organizational maintanance/next authorized repair level as soon as possible.

2-8   Change 1

Preventive MAINTENANCE CHECKS AND SERVICES (PMCS) TABLE

B = Before Operation   D = During Operation   A = After Operation

Item no.	Interval B D A	ITEM TO BE INSPECTED Procedure	Equipment is NOT READY/AVAILABLE IF:
1	•	EQUIPMENT. Check the additional authorizad equipment for completeness and serviceability (app C).	
2	•	9MM PISTOL. Visually inspect the entire pistol for damaged or missing components.	

There are damaged or missing components. ◄

2-9

PREVENTIVE MAINTENANCE CHECKS AND SERVICES (PMCS) (CONT)

B = Before Operation   D = During Operation   A = After Operation

Item no.	Interval B D A	ITEM TO BE INSPECTED Procedure	Equipment is NOT READY/AVAILABLE IF:
3	•	DECOCKING/SAFETY LEVER.	

a. Place decocking/safety lever in safe (down) position, pull trigger. Hammer should not move.

Hammer moves to the rear. ◄

b. Place decocking/safety lever in fire (up) position (see p 2-11). Pull trigger fully to the rear. Hammer should cycle.

Hammer does not move to the rear. ◄

c. Manually cock hammer. Place decocking/safety lever in safe (down) position. Hammer should fall.

Hammer remains cocked. ◄

2-10   Change 1

PREVENTIVE MAINTENANCE CHECKS AND SERVICES (PMCS) (CONT)

B = Before Operation   D = During Operation   A = After Operation

Item no.	Interval B D A	ITEM TO BE INSPECTED Procedure	Equipment is NOT READY/AVAILABLE IF:
4	•	DECOCKING/SAFETY LEVER SLIDE STOP. Place decocking/safety lever in fire (up) position. Pull slide fully to rear while pushing up on slide stop. Slide should lock to the rear. Slide stop does not lock and slide returns to forward position. SLIDE STOP	

Change 1   2-11

PREVENTIVE MAINTENANCE CHECKS AND SERVICES (PMCS) (CONT)

B = Before Operation   D = During Operation   A = After Operation

Item no.	Interval B D A	ITEM TO BE INSPECTED Procedure	Equipment is NOT READY/AVAILABLE IF:
5	•	MAGAZINE CATCH ASSEMBLY. a. Insert an empty magazine into the magazine well until fully seated in place. Hold pistol in an upright position. Magazine should remain seated. Magazine falls free. b. Prepare to catch magazine. Depress magazine release button. Magazine should fall free. Magazine does not fall free. MAGAZINE RELEASE BUTTON	

2-12

PREVENTIVE MAINTENANCE CHECKS AND SERVICES (PMCS) (CONT)

B = Before Operation   D = During Operation   A = After Operation

Item no.	Interval B	D	A	ITEM TO BE INSPECTED Procedure	Equipment is NOT READY/AVAILABLE IF:
6	•			**MAGAZINE ASSEMBLY**	

FOLLOWER

MAGAZINE ASSEMBLY

   a. Visually inspect for missing or damaged parts. Magazine should be free of damage.

> There are missing or damaged parts. ◄

   b. Depress follower with finger and release. Follower should move freely.

> Follower does not return to uppermost position. ◄

   c. Insert empty magazine into the magazine well until fully seated in place. Hold pistol in an upright position. Magazine should remain seated.

> Magazine falls free. ◄

2-13

PREVENTIVE MAINTENANCE CHECKS AND SERVICES (PMCS) (CONT)

B = Before Operation   D = During Operation   A = After Operation

Item no.	Interval B	D	A	ITEM TO BE INSPECTED Procedure	Equipment is NOT READY/AVAILABLE IF:
7	•	•			
8			•		

WARNING

Be sure to clear weapon before performing during PMCS.

PERIODIC INSPECTION OF PISTOL AND MAGAZINE.

   a. Periodically inspect pistol and magazine to ensure that they are clean.

   b. Clean and lubricate pistol and magazine daily, when in use (p 3-21).

9MM PISTOL. Disassemble pistol (p 3-13). Clean and lubricate according to instructions (p 3-21). Inspect all parts for serviceability.

> Any parts require replacement. ◄

PREVENTIVE MAINTENANCE CHECKS AND SERVICES   (PMCS) (CONT)

B = Before Operation   D = During Operation   A = After Operation

Item no.	Interval B	Interval D	Interval A	ITEM TO BE INSPECTED Procedure	Equipment is NOT READY/AVAILABLE IF:
9			•	MAGAZINE ASSEMBLY. Disassemble magazine (p 3-17). Clean and lubricate according to instructions (p 3-21). Inspect all parts for Serviceability.	
				Any parts require replacement.	
10	•		•	Perform Safety/Function Check (p 3-32).	
11	•	•	•	Report all damaged or missing parts to organizational maintenance/next authorized repair level.	

2-15

TM 9-1005-317-10

Section III. OPERATION UNDER USUAL CONDITIONS.

WARNING

Always keep your finger away from the trigger unless you intend to fire. Make sure the pistol is not already loaded by inspecting the magazine and chamber.

For safety considerations, the hammer should always be lowered to the fully down position by depressing the decocking/safety lever.

2-5. PREPARATION FOR FIRING. Perform your Before Operation (B) PMCS.

2-6. LOADING THE MAGAZINE.

a. Hold the magazine (1) in one hand. With the other hand place a cartridge (2) on the follower (3) in front of the lips (4). Press down and slide the cartridge completely back under the lips.

b. Repeat step a above until the magazine is fully loaded (15 cartridges). Holes (5) on the back side of the magazine allow for visual counting of cartridges.

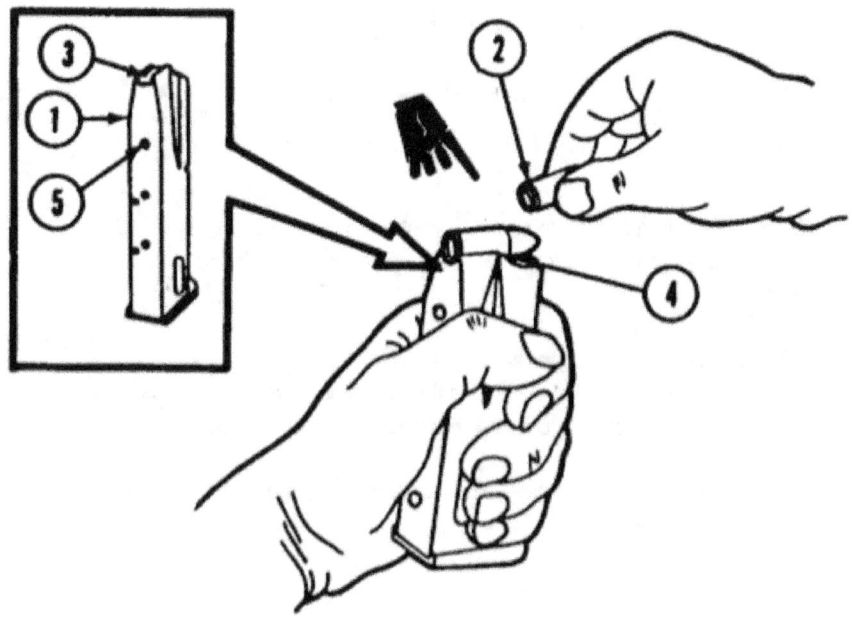

TM 9-1005-317-1O

2-7. LOADING THE PISTOL.

WARNING

The M9 pistol incorporates single and double action modes of fire. Anytime the trigger is pulled with the decocking/safety lever in the fire (up) position and a round in the chamber, the pistol will firs from the hammer down, half cock or full cock positions.

NOTE

The decocking/safety lever should be in the down position which indicates the pistol is in a safe condition before loading.

a. Insert the loaded magazine (1) into the magazine well (2) of the pistol until a click of the magazine catch is heard. This will ensure proper catch engagament.

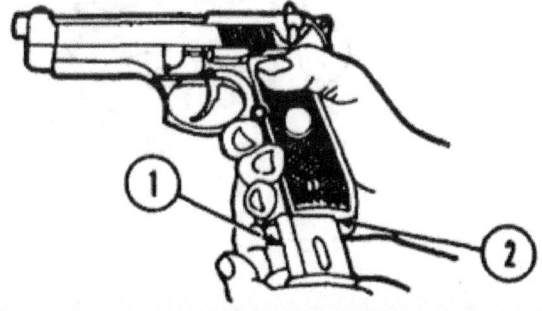

b. With the pistol pointing in a safe direction, grasp the serrated portion of the slide and retract the slide to the rear. Releasing the slide will strip a cartridge from the magazine and chamber it.

WARNING

The pistol is now loaded.

NOTE

For double action firing, the hammer must be in the forward or half cocked position. Squeezing the trigger will cock and release the hammer, firing the pistol.

After the first shot the pistol will continually fire in the single action mode. When the hammer is in the down position, the single action firing mode can be accomplished by manually cocking the hammer with the thumb.

When the last round in the magazine has been fired, the slide will remain to the rear.

2-19

TM 9-1005-317-10

2-8. WHEN READY TO FIRE.

a. Release the decocking/safety lever by rotating the decocking/safety lever (1) to the fully up ward position with the thumb.

WARNING

The pistol is now ready to fire.

b. Aim the pistol at the target.

c. Fire by squeezing the trigger (2).

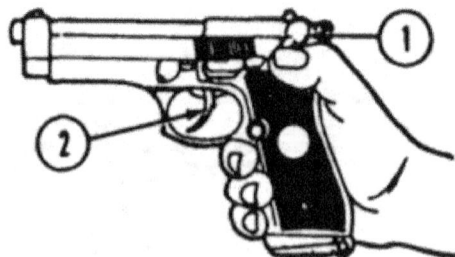

2-9. UNLOADING THE PISTOL.

a. Place decocking/safety lever (1) in "safe" (down) position.

b. Depress the magazine release button (2) to remove the magazine (3) from the pistol.

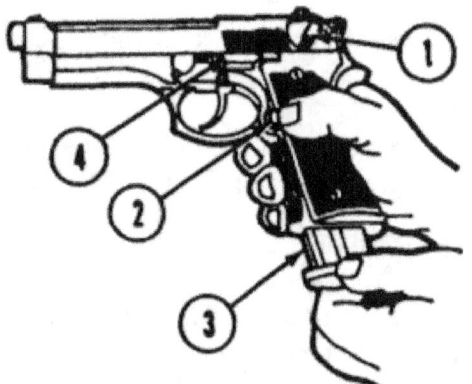

c. With the pistol pointing in e safe direction, grasp the slide narrations and fully retract the slide to remove the chambered cartridge.

d. Lock the slide to the rear using the slide stop (4) and visually inspect chamber to ensure that it is empty.

Change 1   2-21

2-10. UNLOADING THE MAGAZINE.

a. With one hand, hold magazine upright with front end forward. With the thumb firmly press down on the cartridge rim and push forward. As the cartridge moves forward, tip it upward end out with the index finger.

b. Repeat the above step until the magazine is empty.

Section IV. OPERATION UNDER UNUSUAL CONDITIONS.

WARNING

Always keep your finger away from the trigger unless you intend to fire. Make sure the pistol is not already loaded by inspecting the magazine and chamber.

For safety considerations, the hammer should always be lowered to the fully down position by depressing the decocking/safety lever.

CAUTION

If extensive corrosion is found and cleaning does not solve the problem, notify organizational maintenance/next authorized repair level.

NOTE

Unusual conditions are defined as any climatic condition requiring special maintenance of the pistol.

Perform the maintenance outlined for the climate that most applies to your operational area. Refer to page 3-1 for lubrication instructions.

2-11. EXTREME COLD.

a . When operating pistol in extremely cold climates, clean and lubricate the pistol inside at room temperature if possible.

b. Apply a light coat of LAW (item 3, app D) to all functional parts.

c. To prevent freezing, keep the pistol covered when moving from a warm to a cold area. This will allow gradual cooling.

d. Always keep the pistol dry.

e. Do not lay a hot pistol in snow or ice.

2-23

f. Keep ammunition dry; moisture will cause malfunctions. Do not lubricate the ammunition.

g. Always keep snow out of the bore of the barrel. If snow should get into the bore, clean the bore before firing using a swab and cleaning rod.

2-12. HOT, WET CLIMATES.

a. Perform maintenance more frequently. Inspect hidden surfaces for corrosion. If corrosion is found, clean and lubricate.

b. To help prevent corrosion, remove hand prints with a cloth. Dry and lubricatea the pistol with CLP/LSA (items 2 and 4, app D).

c. Check ammunition and magazines frequently for corrosion. Clean the magazine using CLP/LSA and wipe dry with a cloth. If necessary, clean ammunition with a dry cloth.

d. Always keep mud out of the bore of the barrel. If mud should get into the bore, clean the bore before firing using a swab and cleaning rod.

2-13. HOT, DRY CLIMATES.

a. Dust and sand will get into pistol and cause malfunctions and excessive wear on component contact surfaces during firing. Keep pistol covered when possible.

b. Corrosion is less likely to form on metal parts in a dry climate. Therefore, lightly lubricate internal working surfaces only with CLP/LSA. Do not lubricate external parts of the pistol. Wipe any excess lubricant from exposed surfaces. Do not lubricate internal components of magazine.

2-14. HEAVY RAIN AND FORDING OPERATIONS - ALL CLIMATES.

a. Perform maintenance in accordance with the appropriate climatic conditions.

b. Always attempt to keep pistol dry.

c. Always drain any water from barrel prior to firing. Dry the bore with a swab and cleaning rod.

d. Lightly lube the bore and chamber.   Generously lube internal and external surfaces of the pistol with CLP/LSA.

Section V. EMERGENCY PROCEDURES.

2-15. IMMEDIATE ACTION.

Immediate action is the prompt action taken by the user to correct a stoppage. The procedure for applying immediate action should become instinctive to the user, without the user attempting to discover the cause. It is important that the user apply immediate action instinctively to correct a stoppage.

WARNING

During the following procedures always keep the pistol pointed in a safe direction.

1. When the slide (1) is fully forward and the pistol fails to fire, apply immediate action as follows:

   a. Ensure that decocking/safety lever is in the fire (up) position.

   b. In a tactical situation, if the pistol does not fire, ensure that the magazine is fully seated, retract the slide to the rear and release.

   c. Squeeze the trigger (2).

   d. In a non-tactical situation, clear/unload the pistol and refer to paragraph
   3.

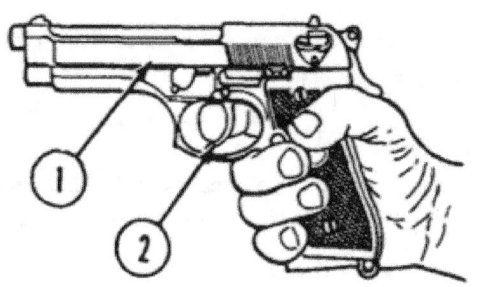

   e. If the pistol still does not fire, remove the magazine and retract the slide to eject the chambered cartridge. Insert a new magazine, retract the slide and release to chamber another cartridge.

   f. Squeeze the trigger.

   g. If the pistol still does not fire, replete the ammunition.

   h. If the pistol still does not fire, clear/unload the pistol and refer to paragraph 3.

WARNING

During the following procedures always keep the pistol pointed in a safe direction.

2. When the slide is not fully seated forward, remove finger from the trigger. With the other hand, attempt to push the slide fully forward. If the slide will not move forward, proceed as follows:

   a. Place decocking/safety lever in safe (down) position.

   b. Remove magazine.

c. Grasp the slide and retract to the rear, locking it with the slide stop.

d. Inspect the chamber and bore and remove any obstructions.

e. Insert another loaded magazine into the pistol.

f. Release slide.

g. Place decocking/safety lever in fire (up) position, aim and attempt to fire,

WARNING

If a round has been assembled without powder (a faulty manufactur ing process), the primer alone has enough power to expel the bullet from the case to lodge in the bore, A bullet lodged in the bore will cause destruction of the pistol if another round is fired, and will also cause personal injury.

3. If the pistol does not fire after the application of immediate action (para 1 and 2 above), a detailed inspection should be made to determine the cause of the stoppage (see Troubleshooting Procedures, Chapter 3). If the cause cannot be determined by the operator, evacuate the pistol to organizational maintenance/next authorized repair level.

2-28   Change 3

CHAPTER 3
MAINTENANCE INSTRUCTIONS

Section I. LUBRICATION INSTRUCTIONS

3-1. LUBE GUIDE.

NOTE

The Instructions In this section are mandatory.

a. CLP, LSA, and LAW are the only lubricants authorized for this pistol.

b. CLP and LSA can be used interchangeably.

c. Remove excess lubricant from the bore before firing.

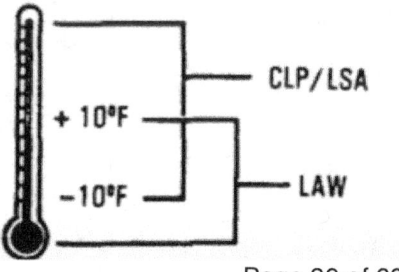

3-1

d. Light coat is defined as a film barely visible to the eye.

e. Generously lubed is defined as heavy enough to be spread with the finger.

For further lubrication instructions, sea Cleaning and Lubrication (p 3-21).

Section II. TROUBLESHOOTING PROCEDURES.

3-2. TROUBLESHOOTING.

a. The table lists the common malfunctions which you may find during the operation or maintenance of the M9 pistol end its components. You should perform the tests/inspections and corrective actions in the order listed.

b. This manual cannot list all malfunctions that may occur, nor all tests or inspections and corrective actions. If a malfunction is not listed or is not corrected by listed corrective actions, evacuate the pistol to organizational maintanance/next authorized repair level.

WARNING

Before performing any of the troubleshooting procedures, make sure the pistol is clear/unloaded.

3-2

NOTE

In this table, evacuate to Organizational Maintenance also means evacuate to the next higher level of maintenance.

TROUBLESHOOTING TABLE

MALFUNCTION
TEST OR INSPECTION
CORRECTIVE ACTION

1. AMMUNITION DOES NOT FEED.

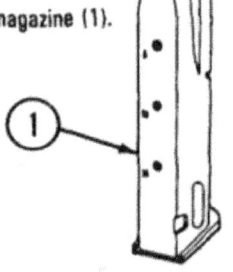

Step 1. Check for improperly positioned top cartridge in magazine (1).

Reload magazine.

Step 2. Check for dirty or rusty magazine.

Clean and lubricate magazine (p 3-21).

Step 3. Check for improper assembly of magazine.

Correctly assemble magazine (p 3-31).

3-3

TROUBLESHOOTING TABLE (cont)

MALFUNCTION
      TEST OR INSPECTION
          CORRECTIVE ACTION

Step 4. Check for broken, damaged or bent parts in magazine.

    Replace magazine.

Step 5. Check for dirty or damaged ammunition.

    Clean or replace ammunition.

Step 6. Check pistol for damaged or broken parts.

    Evacuate pistol to Organizational Maintenance.

2. AMMUNITION DOES NOT CHAMBER.

Step 1. Check for dirty or damaged ammunition.

    Clean or replace ammunition.

TROUBLESHOOTING TABLE (cont)

MALFUNCTION
    TEST OR INSPECTION
        CORRECTIVE ACTION

Step 2. Check for any obstructions or dirt in the chamber (2) and bore.

    Clean chamber and bore (p 3-21).

Step 3. Check for damaged or broken recoil spring (3).

    Evacuate pistol to Organizational Maintenance.

TROUBLESHOOTING TABLE (cont)

MALFUNCTION
     TEST OR INSPECTION
          CORRECTIVE ACTION

3. SLIDE DOES NOT LOCK FULLY FORWARD.

Step 1. Check for dirty locking block and lugs.

Clean pistol (p 3-21).

Step 2. Check all operating parts for lack of lubrication.

Lubricate pistol (p 3-21).

Step 3. Check for broken or damaged locking block and lugs.

Evacuate pistol to Organizational Maintenance.

Step 4. Check for damaged or broken recoil spring.

Evacuate pistol to Organizational Maintenance.

3-6

MALFUNCTION
TEST OR INSPECTION
CORRECTIVE ACTION

Step 5. Chock for damaged or burred slide.

Evacuate pistol to Organizational Maintenance.

4. PISTOL DOES NOT FIRE.

Step 1. Check decocking/safety lever.

Place decocking/safety lever in fire (up) position.

Step 2. Check for faulty ammunition.

Replace ammunition.

Step 3. Check ammunition for fight or no firing pin indent of primer,

Evacuate pistol to Organizational Maintenance.

Stap 4. Check hammer. Hemmer does not fall.

Evacuate pistol to Organizational Maintenance.

MALFUNCTION
TEST OR INSPECTION
CORRECTIVE ACTION

Step 5. Check for broken firing pin block lever (4).

Evacuate pistol to Organizational Maintenance.

5. SLIDE DOES NOT UNLOCK.

Step 1. Check for faulty ammunition, determined by short recoil.

Check bore and replace ammunition.

Step 2. Check for broken or damaged locking block and lugs.

Evacuate pistol to Organizational Maintenance.

Step 3. Check for damaged or broken slide.

Evacuate pistol to Organizational Maintenance.

TROUBLESHOOTING TABLE (cont)

MALFUNCTION
    TEST OR INSPECTION
        CORRECTIVE ACTION

6. CARTRIDGE DOES NOT EXTRACT.

Step 1. Check chamber (5) for dirt or obstructions.

        Clean chamber and barrel (p 3-21).

Step 2. Check for dirty or corroded ammunition.

        Replace ammunition.

Step 3. Check for pitted or damaged chamber.

        Evacuate pistol to Organizational Maintenance.

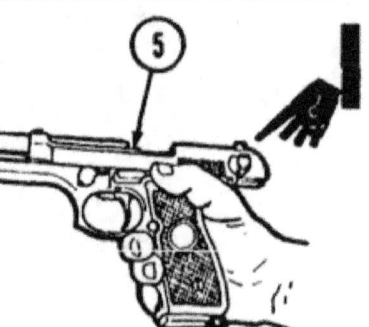

TROUBLESHOOTING TABLE (cont)

MALFUNCTION
    TEST OR INSPECTION
        CORRECTIVE ACTION

Step 4. Check for broken extractor spring by pulling on the front edge of extractor.

        Evacuate pistol to Organizational Maintenance if there is little or no resistance.

Step 5. Check for broken extractor. Check extractor lip to ensure that it is not broken.

        Evacuate pistol to Organizational Maintenance.

7. CARTRIDGE DOES NOT EJECT.

Check for broken ejector (6).

        Evacuate pistol to Organizational Maintenance.

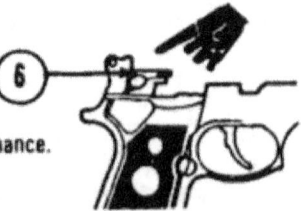

TROUBLESHOOTING TABLE (cont)

MALFUNCTION
    TEST OR INSPECTION
        CORRECTIVE ACTION

---

8. HAMMER DOES NOT COCK WITH DECOCKING/SAFETY LEVER IN FIRE (UP) POSITION.

    No test or inspection.

        Evacuate pistol to Organizational Maintenance.

9. HAMMER DOES NOT DECOCK WITH DECOCKING/SAFETY LEVER IN SAFE (DOWN) POSITION.

    No test or inspection.

        Evacuate pistol to Organizational Maintenance.

10. SLIDE SEPARATES UPON FIRING.

    No test or inspection.

        Evacuate pistol to Organizational Maintenance.

Change 2   3-11/(3-12 blank)

Section III. MAINTENANCE PROCEDURES

3-3. DISASSEMBLY (FIELD STRIPPING).

CAUTION

Dry firing of the pistol is only to be done in conjunction with the function checks in PMCS (ch 2) and/or during training.

Do not allow the hammer to fall with full force by pulling the trigger when the slide is removed as damage to the receiver will occur. If necessary, the hammer should be manually lowered.

Before disassembly, ensure that decocking/safety lever is in the safe (down) position.

NOTE

Disassembly of the M9 pistol beyond field strip (operator) level is not authorized.

Change 1   3-13

1. Clear/unload the pistol (1) (p 2-21).

2. Allow slide (2) to return fully forward.

3-14 Change 1

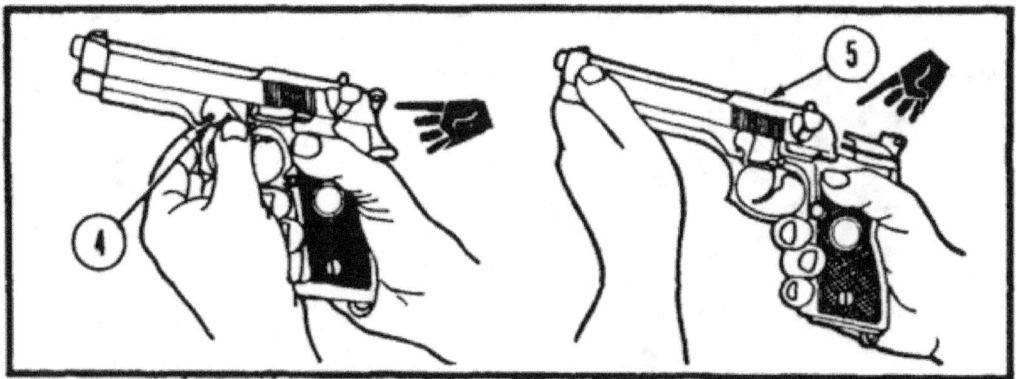

3. Hold pistol in the right hand with muzzle slightly elevated. With forefinger press disassembly lever release button (3), end with thumb rotate disassembly lever (4) downward until it stops.

4. Pull the slide end barrel assembly (5) forward and remove.

WARNING

Use care when removing recoil spring and spring guide. Due to the amount of compression, assembly will be released under spring tension and could cause possible injury to personnel, or become damaged or lost.

Change 1   3-15

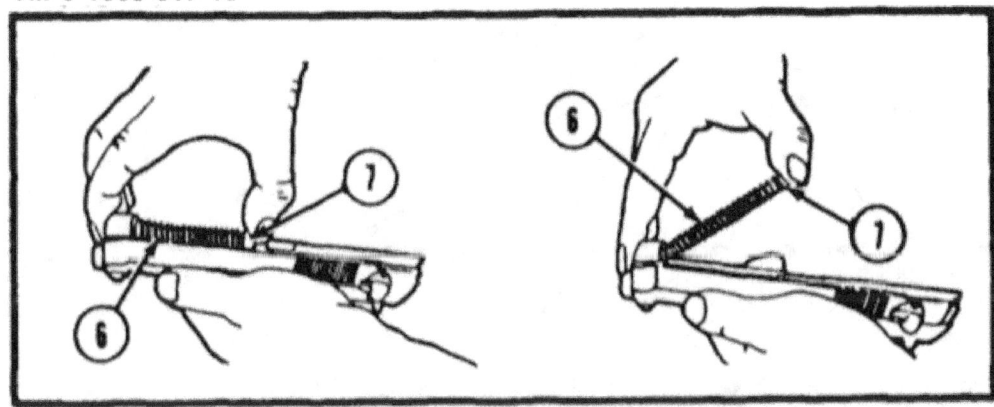

5. Slightly compress recoil spring (6) end spring guide (7), while et the same time lifting and removing recoil spring (6) end spring guide (7). Allow the recoil spring to stretch slowly.

6. Separate recoil spring (6) from spring guide (7).

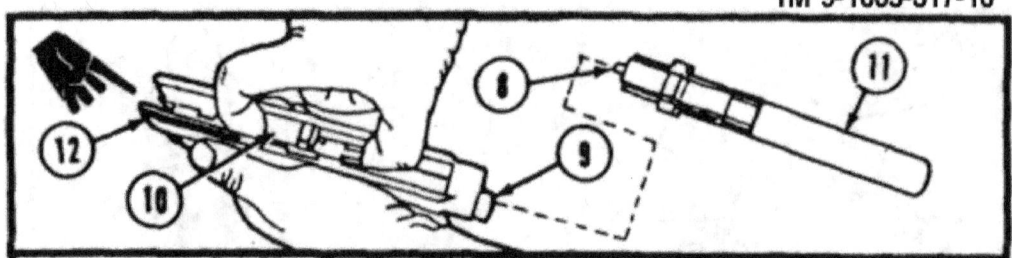

7. Push in on locking block plunger (8) while pushing barrel (9) forward slightly. Lift and remove locking block (10) and barrel assembly (11) from slide (12).

NOTE

Use the following steps to disassemble the magazine.

8. Unload the magazine (p 2-22).

9. Grasp the magazine firmly with the floorplate (1) up and the back of the magazine tube (2) against the palm of the hand.

NOTE

To remove the floorplate, either use the tip of the 9mm round or use the barrel locking block plunger. By depressing the locking block, the locking block plunger will protrude and can be used to assist in removal of the floorplate.

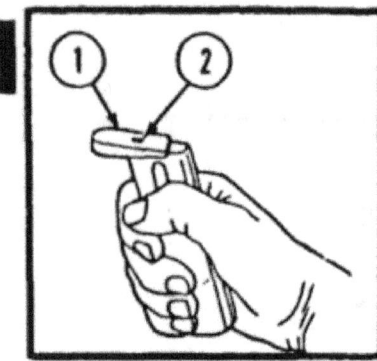
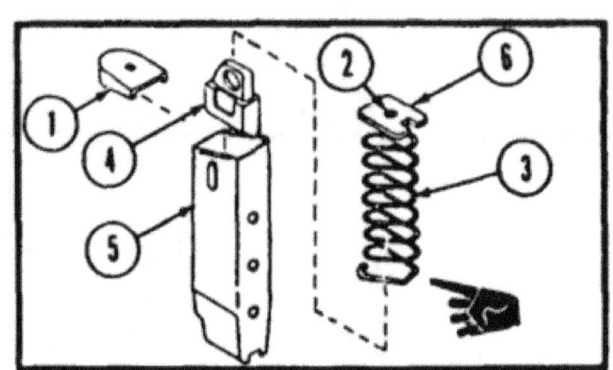

10. Release the floorplate (1) by pushing down on the floorplate retainer stud (2) in the center of the floorplate (1). At the same time, slide the floorplate (1) forward for a short distance using the thumb.

CAUTION

Magazine spring is under slight tension. Use care when removing magazine floorplate.

11. While maintaining the magazine spring pressure with the thumb, remove the floorplate (1) from the magazine.

12. Remove the floorplate retainer and magazine spring (3) and follower (4) from the magazine tube (5). Remove floorplate retainer (6) from magazine spring (3).

NOTE

Disassembly of the M9 pistol beyond field strip (operator] level is not authorized.

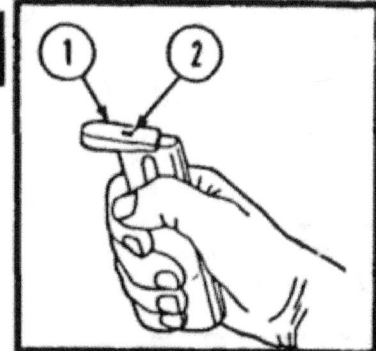
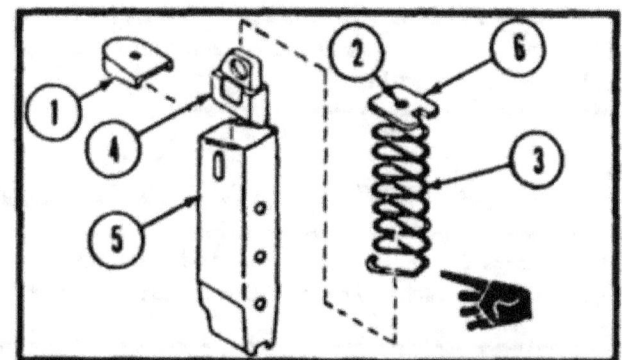

10. Release the floorplate (1) by pushing down on the floorplate retainer stud (2) in the center of the floorplate (1). At the same time, slide the floorplate (1) forward for a short distance using the thumb.

CAUTION

Magazine spring is under slight tension. Use care when removing magazine floorplate.

11. While maintaining the magazine spring pressure with the thumb, remove the floorplate (1) from the magazine.

12. Remove the floorplate retainer and magazine spring (3) and follower (4) from the magazine tube (5). Remove floorplate retainer (6) from magazine spring (3).

NOTE

Disassembly of the M9 pistol beyond field strip (operator] level is not authorized.

3-18   Change 1

3-4. INSPECTION.

NOTE

If faults are found during inspection that cannot be corrected, evacuate pistol to organizational maintenance/next authorized repair level.

a. SLIDE ASSEMBLY (A). Check for free movement of decocking/safety lever (1) and push on firing pin block (2). Check for rear sight (3) looseness. Check for cracks in locking block retaining slot (4).

b. BARREL ASSEMBLY (B). Inspect bore and chamber (5) for pitting or obstructions. Check locking block plunger (6) for free movement of locking block (7). Inspect locking lugs (8) and barrel lugs (9 and 10) for cracks and burrs.

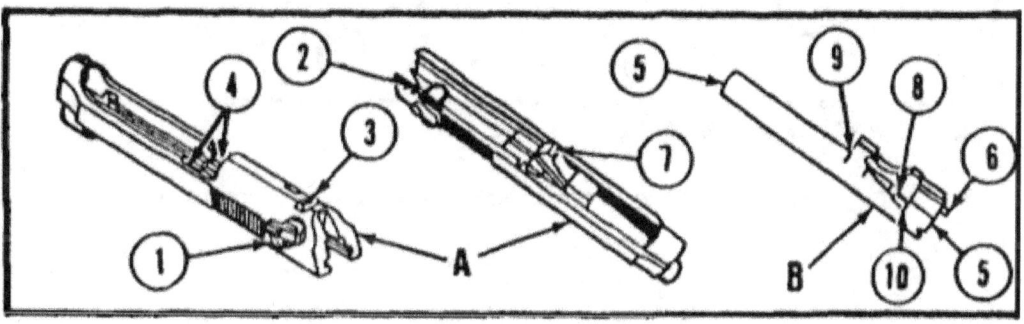

c. RECOIL SPRING AND RECOIL SPRING GUIDE (C). Check recoil spring (1) for damage, Check that it is not bent. Check recoil spring guide (2) for straightness and smoothness. Check to be sure that it is free of cracks and burrs.

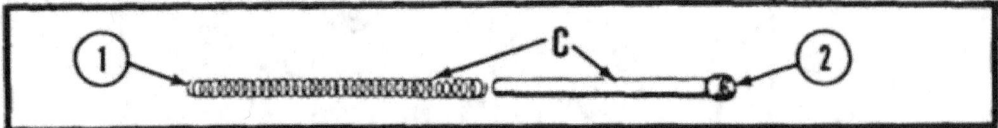

d. RECEIVER ASSEMBLY (D). Check for bends, chips, and cracks. Check for free movement of slide stop (1), and magazine catch assembly (2). Check guide rails (3) for excessive wear, burrs, cracks, or chips.

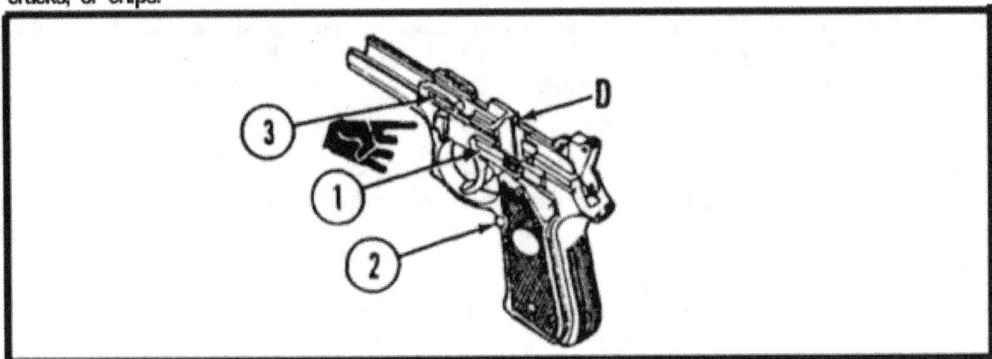

e. MAGAZINE ASSEMBLY Check for spring (1) and follower (2) damage. Ensure that the lips (3) of the magazine are not excessively bent and are free of cracks and burrs. The magazine tube (4) should not be bent or dirty.

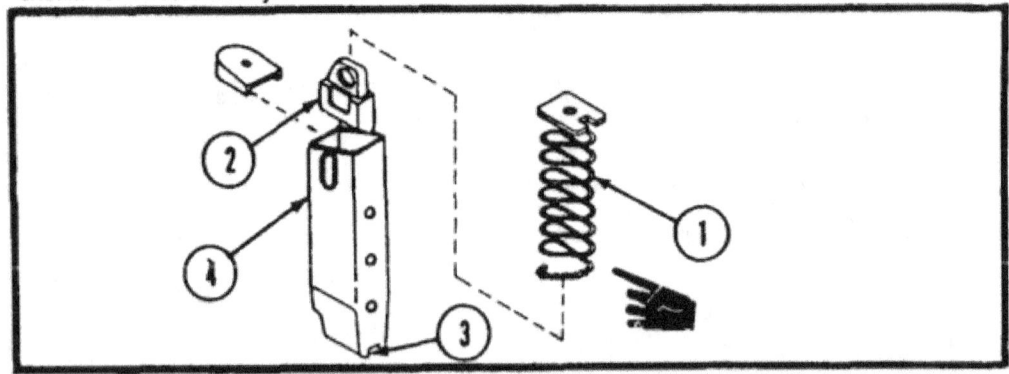

3-5. CLEANING AND LUBRICATION.

CAUTION

Bore brush is for cleaning bore only. Use of bore brush on any other part of the pistol will cause damage.

NOTE

When cleaning, be careful not to lose component parts.

a. SLIDE ASSEMBLY.

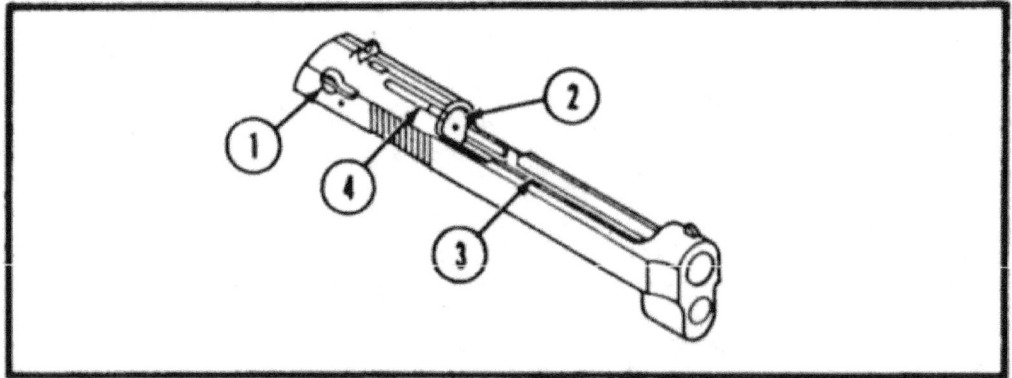

(1) Clean slide assembly with cloth. A soft brush and CLP can assist in removal of excess dirt and carbon buildup. Ensure the decocking/safety lever (1), breech face (2), slide guides (3) and extractor (4) are free of excess dirt and residue.

(2) Wipe dry with a cloth and apply a light coat of CLP/LSA.

3-22   Change 1

b. BARREL ASSEMBLY.

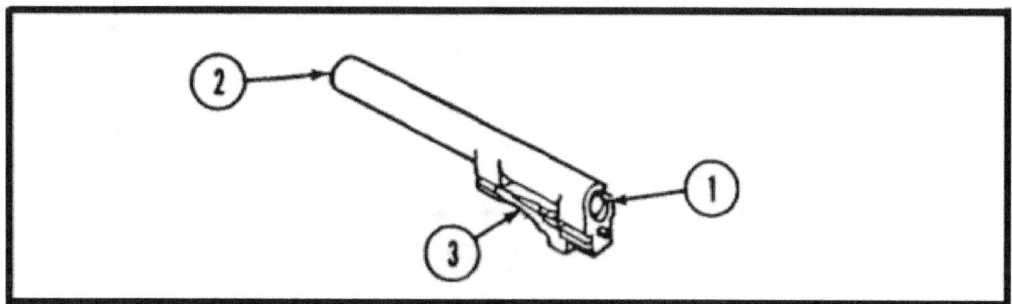

(1) Using cleaning rod, insert cleaning patch soaked with CLP in chamber end of barrel and push out muzzle to remove loose firing residues and soften carbon deposits.

(2) Insert bore brush into chamber end (1) of barrel, making sure it completely clears the muzzle (2) before it is pulled back through the bore Repeat several times to loosen carbon deposits.

(3) Wipe loose carbon deposits from bore with another clean patch soaked with CLP.

Change 3   3-22.1/(3-22.2 blank)

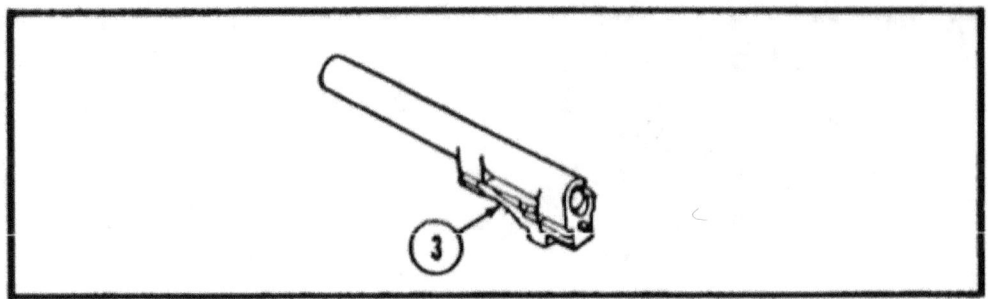

(4) Dry the barrel by pushing a swab through the bore. Repeat as necessary until a clean swab can be observed.

(5) Clean locking block (3) with a soft brush such as toothbrush,

(6) Apply a light coat of CLP/LSA to the barrel bore and chamber area. Also, lubricate the exterior surfaces of the barrel and locking block.

Change 3   3-23

c. RECOIL SPRING AND RECOIL SPRING GUIDE.

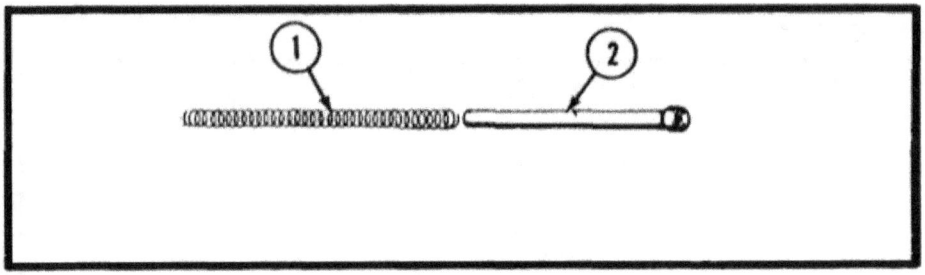

(1) Clean recoil spring (1) and recoil spring guide (2) using CLP and a soft brush or cloth.

(2) After wiping the recoil spring (1) and recoil spring guide (2) clean, apply a light coat of CLP/LSA.

CAUTION

Do not allow the hammer to fall with full force by pulling the trigger when the slide is removed as damage to the receiver will occur. If necessary, the hammer should be manually lowered.

3-24

d. RECEIVER ASSEMBLY.

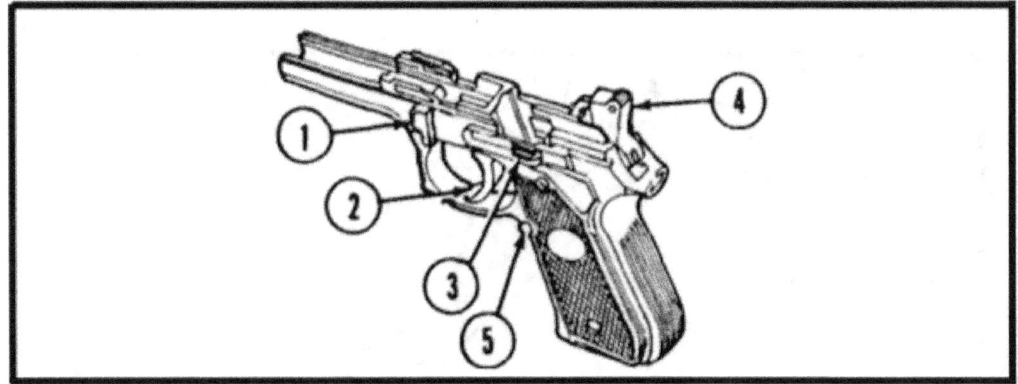

CAUTION

When cleaning the magazine well area, take care not to dislodge the trigger bar spring from the hole provided in the trigger bar and receiver.

(1) Wipe receiver assembly clean with cloth. Use e soft brush for hard to clean areas. Pay special attention to disassembly lever (1), trigger (2), slide stop (3), hammer (4), and magazine release button (5).

(2) Apply a light coat of CLP/LSA.

Change 3   3-25

e. MAGAZINE

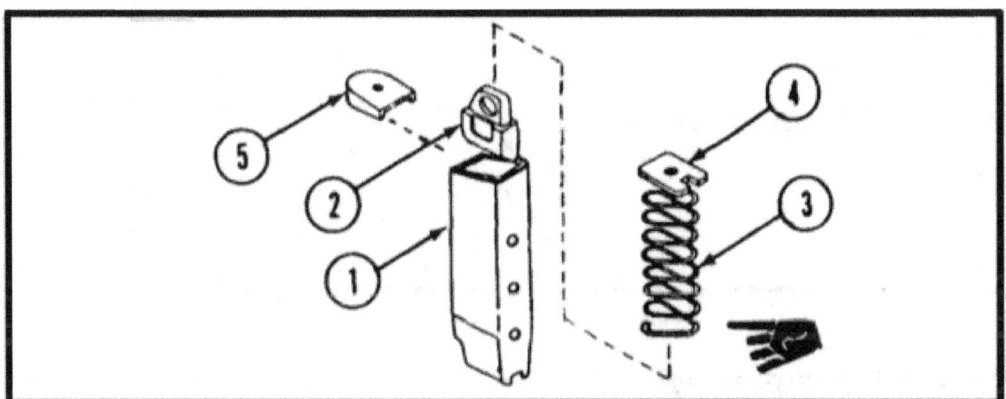

(1) Wipe magazine tube (1) and follower (2) with a cloth. Clean the magazine tube and follower with CLP and a soft brush.

(2) With a cloth, wipe the magazine spring (3), floorplate ratainer (4), and, floorplate (5) clean. Apply a light coat of CLP/LSA.

3-26   Change 1

3-6. REASSEMBLY.

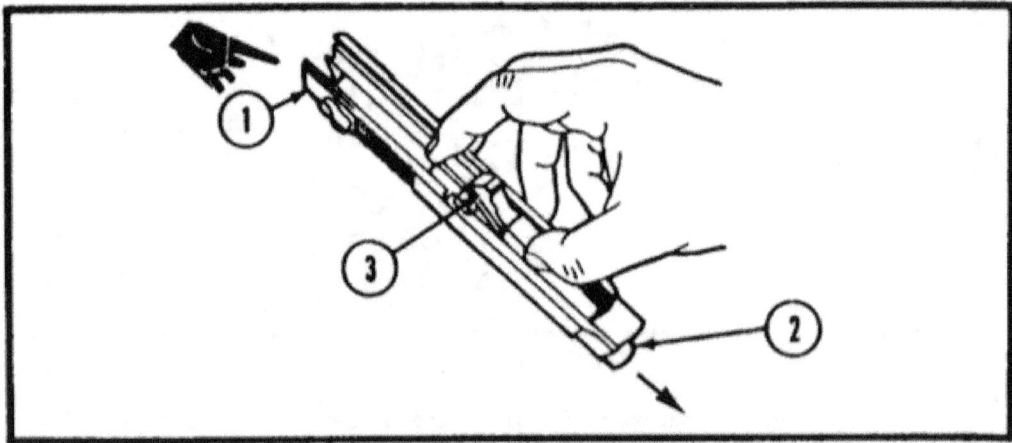

1. Grasp the slide (1) with the bottom facing up. With the other hand grasp the barrel assembly (2) with the locking block (3) facing up.

2. Insert muzzle of the barrel assembly (2) into the forward open and of the slide (1). At the same time lower the rear of the barrel assembly by alining the extractor cutout with the extractor. The locking block will fall into the locked position in the slide.

Change 2   3-27

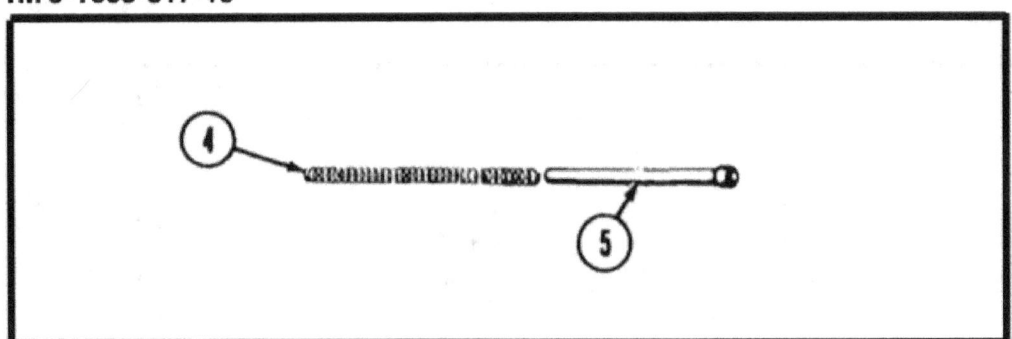

3. Insert recoil spring (4) onto recoil spring guide (5).

CAUTION

During spring insertion, spring tension must be maintained until spring guide is fully seated onto the cutaway on the locking block.

3-28

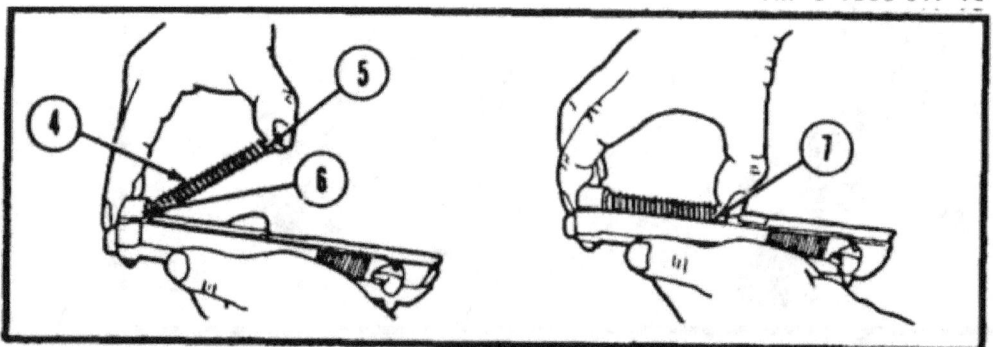

4. Insert and of recoil spring (4) and recoil spring guide (5) into slide recoil spring housing (6). At the same time, compress the recoil spring and lower the spring guide until fully seated onto the locking block cutaway (7).

CAUTION

Be sure hammer is uncocked and firing pin block lover is in the down position. If the hammer is cocked, carefully and manually lower the hammer.

Do not pull trigger while placing the slide onto the receiver.

Before reassembly ensure that decocking/safety lever is in the safe (down) position.

Change 1   3-29

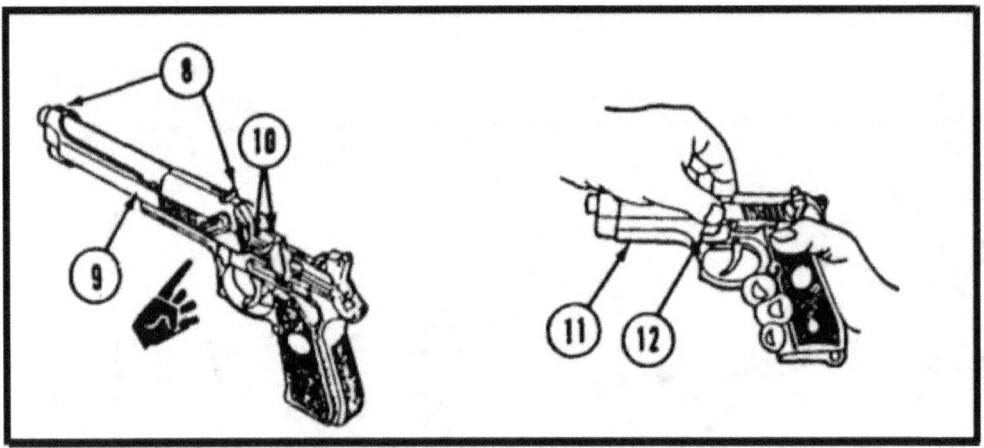

5. Grasp the slide and barrel assembly, sights (8) up, and aline the slide (9) onto the receiver assembly guide rails (10).

6. Push until the rear of the slide (9) is a short distance beyond the rear of the receiver assembly (11) and hold. At the same time, rotate the disassembly latch lever (12) upward. A click indicates a positive lock.

NOTE
Use the following steps to reassemble the magazine.

*U.S.G.P.O. 1989 643-046/00219

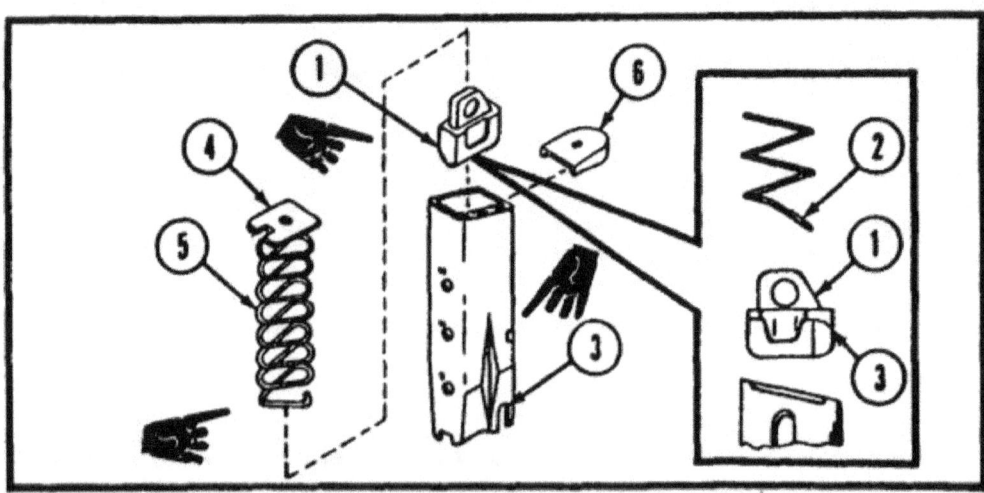

7. Insert the follower (1) into the top coil (2) of the magazine spring. The top coil has an upward and forward pointing end. Ensure that the notches (3) on the follower and magazine tube are on the same side.

8. Insert the magazine spring with follower into magazine tube.

9. Turn the magazine bottom up with the back side against the palm of the hand.

10. Attach and center the floorplate retainer (4) to bottom spring coil.

CAUTION

After insertion, spring tension must be maintained using the thumb.

Do not place lips of magazine tube on a hard surface during reassembly.

11. Push and hold the magazine spring (5) and floorplate retainer (4) down. At the same time, slide floorplate (6) over the side walls until fully seated. This will be indicated by a click.

12. Insert the magazine into the magazine well of the pistol carefully. A click indicates the locked position.

WARNING

Before performing the following safety/function check, clear the pistol and magazine in accordance with the unloading procedures.

3-7. SAFETY/FUNCTION CHECK.

1. Depress the slide stop. Insert an empty magazine into the pistol, and ensure that the magazine catch locks the magazine in place.

2. Retract the slide and release it. The magazine follower should push up on the slide stop, locking the slide to the rear.

3. Depress the magazine release button allowing the magazine to fall free.

4. Ensure the decocking/safety lever is in the safe (down) position. Depress the slide stop allowing the slide to return fully forward. At the same time, the hammer should fell to the full forward position.

5. Squeeze and release trigger. Firing pin block should move up and down, Hammer should not move.

6. Place decocking/safety lever in fire (up) position.

7. Squeeze trigger to check double action. Hammer should cock and fall.

6. Squeeze trigger again and hold to rear. Manually retract and release slide while holding trigger to the rear. Release trigger, click should be heard, hammer should not fall.

9. Squeeze trigger to check single action. Hammer should fall.

10. If the above safety/function checks perform as indicated, pistol is mission ready. If the checks do not perform as indicated, evacuate to organizational maintenance/next authorized repair level.

CHAPTER 4
INTRODUCTION

4-1. AUTHORIZED AMMUNITION.

WARNING

Use any NATO qualified 9-mm ammunition, any U.S. produced M882 ball or any issued ammunition authorized by your service.

Do not fire heavily corroded or dented cartridges, cartridges with loose bullets, or any other defective rounds detected by visual inspection.

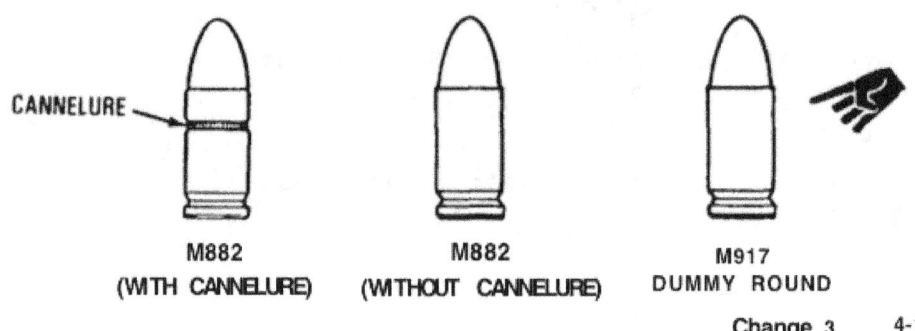

CANNELURE		
M882	M882	M917
(WITH CANNELURE)	(WITHOUT CANNELURE)	DUMMY ROUND

Change 3   4-1

4-2. AMMUNITION WHICH FAILS TO FIRE.

Dispose of any ammunition which fails to firs according to authorized procedures.

4-3. CARE, HANDLING, AND PRESERVATION.

a. Protect ammunition from mud, sand, and water. If the ammunition gets wet or dirty, wipe it off at once with a clean dry cloth. Wipe off light corrosion as soon as it is discovered. Turn in heavily corroded cartridges.

b. Do not expose ammunition to the direct rays of the sun. If the powder is hot, excessive pressure may develop when the pistol is fired.

c. Do not oil or grease ammunition. Dust and other abrasives that collect on greasy ammunition may cause damage to the operating parts of the pistol. Oiled cartridges produce excessive chamber pressure.

4-2

APPENDIX A
REFERENCES

A-1. SCOPE.

This appendix lists all forms, field manuals, technical manuals, tables, regulations, standards, ands miscellaneous publication referenced in this manual.

A-2. TECHNICAL MANUALS.

TM 740-90-1 . . . . Administrative Storage of Equipment
TM 750-244-7 . . . . Procedures for Destruction of Equipment to Prevent Enemy Use
TM 9-1300-206 . . . . Care and Storage of Ammunition

A-3. COMMON TABLE OF ALLOWANCES (CTA).

CTA 50-970 . . . . Expendable/Durable Items (except: Medical, Class V, Repair Parts
and Heraldic Items)

A-4. ARMY REGULATIONS AND PAMPHLETS.

DA PAM 310-1 . . . . Consolidated Index of Army Publications and Blank Forms
DA PAM 738-750 . . . . The Army Maintenance Management System (TAMMS)

A-5. FIELD MANUALS

FM 3-4 . . . . Nuclear, Biological and Chemical (NBC) Protection
FM 3-5. , ... Nuclear, Biological and CHemical (NBC) Decontamination
FM 3-87 . . . . Nuclear, Biological and Chemical (NBC) Reconnaissance and
Decontamination Operations (How to Fight)
FM 21-11 . . . . First Aid for Soldiers
FM 23-35 . . . . Pistols and Revolvers

A-6. FORMS.

DAForm2028 . . . . Recommended Changes to Publications and Blank Forms
NAVMC Form 10772 . . . . Recommended Changes to Publications and Blank Forms
SF 368 . . . . Quality Deficiency Report
DA Form 2404. . . . . Equipment Inspection and Maintenance Worksheet
AFTO Form 22 . . . . Technical Order System Publications Improvement Report and Reply

APPENDIX B
COMPONENTS OF END ITEMS AND BASIC ISSUE ITEMS LISTS

Section I. INTRODUCTION

B-1. SCOPE.

This appendix lists components of end item and basic issue items for the M9 pistol to help you inventory items required for safe and efficient operation.

B-2. GENERAL.

The components of End Item and Basic Issue Items Lists are divided into the following sections

a. Section II. Components of End Item (COEI). Not applicable.

b. Section III. Basic Issue hams (BII). These are the minimum essential items required to place the M9 pistol in operation, to operate it, and to perform emergency repairs. Although shipped separately packaged, BII must be with the M9 pistol during operation and whenever it is transferred between property accounts. This manual is your authority to request/requisition replacement BII, based on Table of Organization and Equipment (TOE)/Modified Table of Organization and Equipment (MTOE) authorization of the end item.

B-1

B-3. EXPLANATION OF COLUMNS.

The following provides an explanation of columns found in the tabular listings

a. **Column (1) - Illustration Number** (Illus Number). This column indicates the number of the illustration in which the item is shown.

b. **Columnn (2) - National Stock Number.** Indicates the National stock number assigned to the item and will be used for requisitioning purposes.

c. **Column (3) - Description.** Indicates the Federal item name and, if required, a minimum description to identify and locate the item. The last line for each item indicates the FSCM (in parentheses) followed by the part number.

d. **Column (4) - Unit of Measure (U/M).** Indicates the measure used in Performing the actual operational/maintenance function. This measure is expressed by a two-character alphabetical abbreviation (e.g., ea, in., pr),

e. **Column (5) - Quantity Required (Qty rqr).** Indicates the quantity of the item authorized t be used with/on the equipment.

Section II. COMPONENTS OF END ITEM

Not applicable.

B-2

Section III. BASIC ISSUE ITEMS

(1) Illus Num- ber	(2) National Stock Number	(3) Description FSCM and Part Number	Usable On Code	(4) U M	(5) Qty rqr
1	N/A	Operator's Manual, M9 9mm Pistol TM 9-1005-317-10		EA	1

B-3/(B-4 blank)

APPENDIX C
ADDITIONAL AUTHORIZATION LIST

Section I. INTRODUCTION

C-1. SCOPE.

This appendix lists additional items you are authorized for the support of the M9 pistol.

C-2. GENERAL.

This list identifies items that do not have to accompany the M9 pistol and that do not have to be turned in with it. These items are all authorized to you by CTA, TOE/MTOE, Table of Distribution Allowances (TDA), or Joint Table of Allowances (JTA).

C-3. EXPLANATION OF LISTING.

National stock numbers, descriptions, and quantities are provided to help you identify end request the additional items you require to support your M9 pistol. The items era listed in alphabetical sequence by item name under the type document (i.e., CTA, TOE, MTOE, TDA, or JTA) which authorizes the items to you.

C-1

Section II. ADDITIONAL AUTHORIZATION LIST

(1) NATIONAL STOCK NUMBER	(2) DESCRIPTION		(3)	(4)
	FSCM & PART NUMBER	USABLE ON CODE	U/M	QTY AUTH
1095-01-194-3343	HOLSTER, PISTOL, HIP, M1 2 (19200) 9388057		EA	1
1095-00-973-2353	HOLSTER, PISTOL, M7 (SHOULDER) (BLACK) (19205) 7791527		EA	1
8465-00-262-5237	LANYARD, INDIVIDUAL (WHITE) (81349) MIL-L-10028		EA	1
8465-00-965-1705	LANYARD, INDIVIDUAL (GREEN) (81349) MIL-L-10028		EA	1
1005-01-204-4376	MAGAZINE, Cartridge (19200) 9346413		EA	1
1005-01-207-5573	POCKET, AMMUNITION, M1 (81337) 2-4-84		EA	1

C-2   Change 1

APPENDIX D
EXPENDABLE/DURABLE SUPPLIES AND MATERIALS LIST

Section I. INTRODUCTION

D-1. SCOPE.

This appendix lists expendable/durable supplies and materials you will need to operate and maintain the pistol. This listing is for informational purposes only and is not authority to requisition the listed items. These items are authorized to you by CTA 50-970, Expendable/Durable Items (except Medical, Class V, Repair Parts, and Heraldic Items) or CTA 8-100, Army Medical Department Expendable/Durable Items.

D-2. EXPLANATION OF COLUMNS.

a. Column (1) - Item Number. This number is assigned to the entry in the listing and is referenced in the narrative instructions to identify the material (e.g., "Use cleaner, lubricant and reservative, CLP item 2, app D").

b. Column (2) - Level. This column identifies the lowest level of maintenance that requires the listed item.

C - Operator/Crew

D-1

D-2. EXPLANATION OF COLUMNS (cont).

c. Column (3) - National Stock Number. This is the National stock number assigned to the item use it to request or requisition the item.

d. Column (4) - Description, Indicates the Federal item name and, IT required, a description to identify the item. The lest line for each item indicates the Federal Supply Code for Manufacturer (FSCM) in parentheses followed by the pert number.

e. Column (5) – Unit of Measure (U/M). Indicates the measure used in performing the actual maintenance function. This measure is expressed by a two-character alphabetical abbreviation (e.g., ea, in., pr). If the unit of measure differs from the unit of issue, requisition the lowest unit of issue that will satisfy your requirements.

Section II. EXPENDABLE/DURABLE SUPPLIES AND MATERIALS LIST

(1) ITEM NUM· BER	(2) LEVEL	(3) NATIONAL STOCK NUMBER	(4) DESCRIPTION	(5) U/M
1	C	1005-00-716-2132	BRUSH, CLEANING SMALL (BORE BRUSH) (19205) 7162132	EA
1.1	C	1005-00-494-6602	BRUSH, CLEANING, SMALL ARMS· (TOOTHBRUSH) (19204) 8448462	EA
2	C	9150-01-102-1473	CLEANER, LUBRICANT PRESERVATIVE (CLP) (81349) MIL-L-63460 1/2 oz btl btl	OZ

Section II. EXPENDABLE/DURABLE SUPPLIES AND MATERIALS LIST (cont)

(1) ITEM NUM· BER	(2 LEVEL	(3) NATIONAL STOCK NUMBER	(4) DESCRIPTION	(5) U/M
3	C	9150-00-292-9689	LUBRICATING OIL, WEAPONS (LAW) (81349) MIL-L-14107 1 qt can	QT
4	C	9150-00-889-3522	LUBRICATING OIL, WEAPONS SEMI-FLUID (LSA) (19204) 8436793 4 oz btl	OZ
5	C	7920-00-205-1711	RAG, WIPING (58536) A-A-531 50 lb bl	LB

Section II. EXPENDABLE/DURABLE SUPPLIES AND MATERIALS LIST (cont)

(1) ITEM NUM- BER	(2) LEVEL	(3) NATIONAL STOCK NUMBER	(4) DESCRIPTION	(5) U/M
6	C	1005-00-556-4102	ROD, CLEANING, M4 (19204) 5564102	EA
7	C	1005-00-288-3565	SWAB, SMALL ARMS PK (19204) 5019316	EA

Change 3   D-5/(D-6 blank)

ALPHABETICAL INDEX

ALPHABETICAL INDEX (cont)

PIN: 058315-003

ALPHABETICAL INDEX (cont)

ALPHABETICAL INDEX (cont)

By Order of the Secretaries of the Army, Navy and Air Force;
Commandants, Marine Corps and Coast Guard:

JOHN A. WICKHAM JR.
General, United States Army
Chief of Staff

Official:

DONALD J. DELANDRO
Brigadier General, United States Army
The Adjutant General

R. E. BROWN
Small Arms Program Manager
Naval Sea Systems Command

CHARLES A. GABRIEL
General, USAF
Chief of Staff

EARL T. O'LOUGHLIN
General, USAF
Commander, Air Force Logistics Command

GEORGE B. CRIST,
Lieutenant General, USMC
Deputy Chief of Staff for Installation and Logistics

N. C. VENZKE
Rear Admiral, USCG
Chief, Office of Operations

TM 9-1005-317-10

Distribution:

Active Army:

To be distributed in accordance with DA Form 12-40C, Operator's Maintenance requirements for Pistol, Caliber .45, Automatic, M1911A1

Marine Corps:

MARCORPS CODE: BN

Navy:

Special

Air Force:

Special

Coast Guard

Special

*U.S. GOVERNMENT PRINTING OFFICE: 1989 - 242-451 (05829)

ARMY TM 9-1005-317-10
NAVY SW 370-AA-OPI-010/9mm
AIR FORCE TO 11W3-3-5-1
MARINE CORPS TM 1005A-10/1
COAST GUARD COMDTINST M8370.6

PISTOL, SEMIAUTOMATIC, 9mm, M9 (1005-01-118-2640)

PIN: 058315-000